Auto Pilot Income

COPYRIGHT © Bart Kohler, CPP December 2016

Printed in the United States of America

All rights reserved by the author. No part of this publication may be reproduced, stored in a retrieval system, or transmitted in any form without the written permission of the author, except for brief quotations in critical reviews or articles.

Bart Kohler, CPP
3286 Highland Park
North Canton OH 44720
yourcpp@gmail.com
855-255-7291

I0391012

Special thanks to:
John Heiermann
Christine Vick
Jada Weiler

Auto Pilot Income

Table of Contents

Introduction 3
Chapter One 4
   Always Selling, Never Gaining Ground 4
Chapter Two 8
   Your Proper Mind Set 8
Chapter Three 16
   Personal Development and Character 16
Chapter Four 19
   Opportunity, Freedom, and Equality 19
Chapter Five 21
   What Is Residual Income And Subscription-Based Income 21
Chapter Six 24
   Getting Started 24
Chapter Seven 28
   Conclusion Or Beginning? 28

Auto Pilot Income

Introduction

In my book you will learn the secrets that I have perfected to earn a passive Multi six figure income every year. For nearly two decades, I have earned money while I slept, went on vacation, or played video games with my son. It's true - while others traded time for money by punching time clocks and commuting in horrendous traffic jams, I stayed in the luxury of my home, comfortably earning a multiple six figure income. How is it possible? By simply following the guidance of my book and applying the talents that you already possess.

First you will learn how to change the way that you look at earning money and ways of producing income. You will be taught the transformation process and the levels of persistence and character that it takes to get the keys to your Auto Pilot Income.

I will provide you with a list of proven business models that many are currently using, as well as map of the pitfalls that you will want to avoid.

Lastly, I will supply you with the tools and trade secrets that you can use immediately, giving you the opportunity to begin your path to financial freedom that most people only dream of. Are you ready?

Chapter One

Always Selling, Never Gaining Ground

I remember as a younger man I had been a salesman, always selling. Once I made a sale, I had to make another and then another and another, just to pay my bills, put gas in the car, and food on the table. The process was grueling and eventually, like many sales people, I began to burn myself out.

After selling everything from sweepers to cars for just five or so years, I was feeling the burn and drain of commission sales. As a salesman, I made it a habit to stay in touch with my customers and call them on a semiannual basis.

One day I made a call to a gentleman about my age, to whom I had sold a car to roughly three years prior. He was a difficult customer, always wanting to come in and test drive cars and constantly negotiating on price. Eventually he bought one. It happened to be the "Loss Leader" for our advertising and the dealership actually lost money on the car. My commission on that sale was one of the smallest that I had ever earned.

I remembered that when I took this man's credit application, I was quite impressed with his income for his age of only 25-years-old. I asked him, "What do you do for a living?" He explained it, but I was young and very naive and it kind of went in one ear and out the other. Still, he made what I considered to be GREAT MONEY, and I made sure that I never lost contact with him. To this day we still bump into each other and he is still doing amazing things.

Auto Pilot Income

About the same time that I began to realize I was getting pretty burned out selling cars, I decided to check in with this well-to-do young businessman to whom I had leased a car three years prior. The conversation went something like this:

"Dave? It's Bart. Your lease on your 94 Pontiac is coming due and I would like to sell you another car."

"Thanks Bart, I actually paid the lease off and am keeping the car for a while."

The conversation moved on.

"How is business? Are you still doing mortgages?" I asked.

"Yes, it's great you should come and join us!" he exclaimed.

That was ALL I needed to hear. Within a week I was at his office, learning a new industry that I really knew nothing about. It turned out that I was pretty bad at certain aspects of the job, but exceptional at others.

Create Your Own Opportunity

As a new commissioned salesperson, I wasn't making near what I wanted and I asked him if I could also work in the telemarketing department for some extra income. But here is the key, I was willing to take LESS in pay than everyone else in the room, with one exception... I wanted a commission of one dollar for every lead that I produced. He agreed, and the exception turned into my inspiration and motivation. I became the best telemarketer in the room consistently. Eventually I was named head of the department and

Auto Pilot Income

the entire company's sales grew by 20 percent. After a few months of proving myself, an incredible opportunity arose.

The owner of the company had a first cousin who was the VP of National Sales for CardService International, a marketing arm for Credit and Debit Card Acceptance or Merchant Services. This business was traditionally handled by bank channels, but with the introduction of the Debit/Check Card, the demand was high and new companies were rapidly emerging.

Nobody at the mortgage company wanted to take on this new task of selling card acceptance to businesses, as they had mortgage leads like never before and wanted to remain earning with the product that they knew best - mortgages.

I, on the other hand, eagerly saw this opportunity as a huge earning potential with a new concept to me - **residual income**. That's right! I could get paid every month off of ONE SALE! Imagine if you sold cars but got paid every mile that someone drove that car, or if you sold a couch and you got paid every time someone sat on it every day for years.

What is residual income? If we look at the definition of Residual Income here is what we may find.

Residual income (also called passive or recurring income) is income that continues to be generated after the initial effort has been expended.

Compare this to what most people focus on earning: linear income, which is "one-shot" compensation or payment in the form of a fee,

Auto Pilot Income

wage, commission or salary. I like to say trading time for dollars. Pretty simple right?

The problem with trading time for dollars is that we quickly run out of hours and cannot get paid enough per hour to really get ahead.

Now that you understand what residual income is, are you ready to begin learning different ways to capture yours right now? Follow the steps of this book and begin changing your life TODAY!

Chapter Two

Your Proper Mind Set

Belief

Seeing is believing. Most people would agree with that statement, right? It sounds good. You have to actually see something and witness it for it to be real, right? Actually that is NOT true. Look at it from this perspective. **Believing is Seeing**!

Follow me here. We must first have a thought before we can put anything into action. When you woke up this morning to get out of bed, your mind had to first believe that your legs would support your body BEFORE you stood on your feet. Before any ACTION there must first be a thought.

Maybe you have heard this old saying... **"Thoughts become actions, actions become habits, habits become your character and your character becomes your destiny. "**

If we can control our mind set we can control our destiny. Seems simple enough, right? We must look at our future in a super positive light, set goals, and take the necessary steps to achieve those goals. Belief in our abilities, resources, and mission are crucial in obtaining success of any measure.

We must erase negativity and replace it with powerful thoughts of confidence and belief. Belief. Belief. Belief. You must first believe.

Now what are you believing for? What is your vision or mission? Close your eyes and see an IMAGE of your success. Imagine the business model or method that you would use to help get you there. That image that you create becomes your vision. Vision is something that is in you, a deep desire that drives your belief. Vision can be defined like this,

Something that can be seen.

Once we can see something in our mind. A reality begins to form and we actually can see ourselves doing what it is that we are thinking about and then acting on it. Swinging that golf club, climbing that mountain, or - for some of us - it may be some of the simple things in life like getting the laundry done or mowing the grass. Everything we do needs a vision for it to form in the mind and begin to become a reality. Once we have our vision alive we must feed it. We have to begin to talk about it and develop it and grow it in our mind. As we do, we can add to our dream. Use your IMAGination to stretch the limits of your vision and to test and refine the vision. All of this is necessary to achieve these missions and goals in our lives. The bigger the vision or dream, the more you need to feed and develop that dream. It takes far more planning to build a house than a shack.

Battle In The Mind

As we discuss creating a positive Vision, we must always remember to win the "Battlefield of the MIND." Good and Evil, Right and Wrong, Angels and Demons whatever you want to use to set up these two conflicting forces in your mind is up to you, but we must realize that they are real and they do exist. After all, we must spend our time thinking about something, right? So many people spend so much time worrying about things that never even happen and they dwell on the negative things in life. They think things like, "Oh, I will never have a enough money to do that or live there. I am just not smart enough to go to school or learn something new. My health isn't great and I am not physically capable to accomplish that." Well if that is what you believe that is what will most likely occur.

Where the mind goes, the body follows. You MUST accomplish in your mind the task you wish to accomplish, the person you wish to become, and the things you wish to possess before anything is possible. Remember the story of the King and the Fool competing in our brain? Whichever one we feed more, listen to more, and reason with, we tend to become.

You Can Control Your Thoughts

Try this exercise with me. Close your eyes and picture yourself in a very happy place., Maybe it is in the sun on the beach next to someone you love. Maybe it is on top of a mountain all by yourself. Take this moment now and just THINK on that place... Did you do that? If you did, then we have just proven that YOU can control your thoughts and think about something that you want to think about.

Now whenever you catch yourself worrying, angry or afraid, remember that you have the POWER to control your own thoughts. Feed the KING inside of you and become a KING. STARVE the FOOL and he will die or go away. Like any other muscle or good habit we must practice it, exercise it, and train it so it will become stronger and more proficient. Practicing positive thinking and always believing for the very best will become a habit and will also spill over onto those around you. After all, we have proven that you can think about whatever you want, so why think about something that will make you sick, afraid, or angry. This may not be as easy as it sounds for some of us at first, but I promise if you practice this and exercise positive thoughts, it will become a tool that you will use for a lifetime. Believe Me.

Talk About Your Vision

Jesse Duplantis says "if you aren't talking about your vision, your vision is going talk about you."

Be persistent in the process. Even though it is NOT reality YET, we must remain possessive of OUR vision and take ownership of it, like a child that you raise up. Have you ever heard the expression, "This is your baby" before? You must be persistent.

When I think of persistence it reminds me of my son John. When he was a little boy he so badly wanted a pet. We tried dogs and cats and he was allergic to them and we never had great success with owning furry pets. However, John had a belief that he would care for a pet, and vision of a pet without fur and so John wanted a SNAKE! First I noticed books coming home from the library about snakes and reptiles. The next sign was him talking to me about snakes and how great they are, and demonstrating his knowledge and interest on the subject. Finally, one day he worked up enough nerve to say, "Dad, can I have a snake?"

"WHAT?" I thought. "A snake? NO way John. We don't have anywhere to put it, what and how will you feed it? How will you give it water or keep it warm? And I don't even know where to get a snake. I am not buying you a snake."

Auto Pilot Income

He is a great kid so he accepted what I had to say without complaining, but my refusal to allow him to have a snake just went in one ear and out the other. He had his vision and he was persistent in his belief. Over the next few weeks he began to tell me how he would feed his snake and where he could buy food if he had a hard time finding food, and he obtained a cage and a water bowl and told me how we could heat the cage with a warming pad and a lamp. This young man had developed in his mind every stinking detail about his life with that snake that didn't even exist yet.

So, being the wise old man that I am I said, "Tell you what buddy, if you can catch a snake and save him from my lawn mower, you can keep him." I never believed in a million years that little boy of only about 10 years old would catch a snake. But every day he would come home from school, do his homework and then ask me, "Dad, can I go out in the yard and look for my snake?" Persistence. Persistence. Persistence. He was so driven in his mind that one day he actually caught that snake. I will never forget the day, I heard, "Dad, dad come quick! I got my snake!"

Well sure enough, he did get a snake who he named "Bob." The snake lived with us for a few years and got too big for the habitat that we created for him with all that great care he received. One day he was big enough to be put back out in the yard, and to this day I think Bob is still roaming in our rock wall in the back yard, and is much too big for me to accidentally harm with my mower.

Now, you may ask, why am I telling you this story. **Persistence** and **patience** made John's dream of having a pet come true.

Auto Pilot Income

I want to talk just a bit about patience because it is so important. Patience allows us to keep the vision alive through the difficult times during the pregnancy of our vision. I say pregnancy because that is what we are doing dreaming and creating our vision. We are giving life to something that we love and that we are believing for. We are nurturing it, and carrying it along until one day it becomes a reality. Alive the whole time, but not yet realized, we sometimes grow weary and can lose hope. Stay patient. We have a saying in our family...delay is not denial. Be patient and persistent and one day you will deliver your dream. This reminds me of another story.

Persistent Person and the Quitter

Once there were two people hired in the sales department for this large company. They worked hard to gain the knowledge of the products, and they trained for months on how to sign customers up for service.

Finally the day came for them to begin visiting every business owner in this small town one by one. So they headed out together and began calling on businesses. They would go in and ask to speak to the owner and they would be told that the owner stepped out or the owner is away for the day. Every single place that they went, it seemed the business owner had something to do that day. Finally the one salesperson said to the other, Forget this job! we will never make a sale. This is crazy!"

The persistent positive salesperson urged the colleague to continue on. He told the colleague that they had come too far and trained so many weeks and long hours.

Auto Pilot Income

The negative colleague argued that the territory was bad. "We will never find a business owner around here," he said

The positive persistent person said, "Look ahead friend. There is a big business with lots of cars parked outside. Let's go see if we can find a business owner in there."

The negative person just shook their head and said, "That place is too busy. The owner will never take time to see us even if they are there. I give up, I quit! "

Well it was many years until one day those two saw each other again. They smiled and exchanged warm greetings like old friends do. The persistent person asked the person who quit how things were going, the quitter responded with "Things have been tough. I never seemed to find the right job, and my bosses always had it out for me. Nobody will pay me what I'm worth. I am still looking for the right job."

The quitter then asked the persistent salesperson, "Whatever happened to you?"

"Well, I actually became head of the sales department. Do you remember the day that you quit? Well I decided to go to the next business... the big building with all of the cars in the parking lot? Do you know it turned out that the big building was a party center, and they were hosting the town's annual business owners meeting, open to the public? That day I bought a ticket, went in, ate lunch, and met with every business owner in town in just a few hours. I made some good friends and have had the pleasure of helping many of the businesses in this town. I have gotten to know them and their families and have become part of the community. Things just couldn't be better."

Quotes to remember:

"It's hard to beat a man that doesn't give up." - Babe Ruth

"A man can fail many times, but he isn't a failure until he begins to blame somebody else." - John Burroughs

Chapter Three

Personal Development and Character

The Keys

This is a book about creating an **Auto Pilot Income**, but I have to take a few moments and discuss personal development and character a bit more. I like to define character as, what you would do when nobody is watching. If you would move your game piece during a game when no one is watching, or change your score on your golf card then then that would make you a cheater. Now we focus on positive things in this book so we won't dwell on poor character but I had to give an example.

A pastor friend of mine, no names please, Dana Gammill of Cathedral of Life Church in Canton, Ohio, once told this story of a young toddler always wanting the keys to the car to play with or be preoccupied with like toddlers do. Of course toddlers cannot even begin to learn how to drive, but they want those keys. As the child grows up he may have chores of washing the car and learning to care for the car like checking the tire pressure and the fluid levels. These are steps of personal development that teach the child how to respect and be invested in that car. Eventually that child turns of age, begins driving lessons and takes the necessary tests by the state to obtain a license to drive. Finally that grand finale moment arrives and those keys that the toddler was once so fond of will now be passed on to this new grown wonderful person of character. Pastor Dana says when your character matches the call, you get the keys. GOOD Character, doing something right or good even though NO ONE is looking is good or right character. We must strive to be highly developed people of good and right character. After all if you are going to possess the valuable resource of **Auto Pilot Income** people will likely support you and continue to support you if you are a person of Good or Right Character. Remember that even when we think no one is watching, they probably are. But you will find like we said in the chapter on Mind Set that once you sow a thought you reap an action, sow an action reap a habit, sow a habit reap a character, sow a character reap a destiny. That was taught to me by another good man Named Greg Laurie. Work hard at developing good thoughts, actions, habits, and character, and you will be developed into someone with a great destiny I am sure.

Transformation

Changing into something that you are NOT is a process, it is a transformation. You must understand that changes are going to take place if you are to fulfill your desire of achieving a passive **Auto Pilot Income**. Some of the aspects of the change may be a little difficult or challenging. Others around us will begin to see these changes taking effect in us and they may be supportive or combative to our new attitude and position of who we are and what we want to become.

Remember that a butterfly was once just a worm and now is something completely different than it was before. It has abilities and freedoms that once would have seemed impossible. I am not saying that you are going to transform into a flying human, but in a sense you will be completely different once you gain the independence of your **Auto Pilot Income**. You will have freedoms only dreamed about and things that as a worm seemed impossible. Remember haters are going to hate and many people will not be in

Auto Pilot Income

your corner. Try to surround yourself with those that will embrace your dream or better yet, surround yourself by those who will take an active part in it.

Something very important that you have probably heard before is Never Say Can't. Remove the C word from your vocabulary. It is destructive to your goal and is very damaging to your vision. Stay filled with the Spirit of CAN and WILL and remove the negativity from your life and things will begin to transform.

Chapter Four

Opportunity, Freedom, and Equality

We are all so fortunate to live in a place and time where people have opportunities. No one told me that I can't start a business, because of my religion, my race, my sexual orientation, or even my height. Now there are people out there who are thinking, life is NOT equal, life is not fair. In this book we focus on the positives.

Yes it is true, not everyone has equal resources but the opportunity is there, and we are free to make our own choices.

Actually, true equality cannot exist where there is freedom. A good example of that is the game of monopoly, where we all start out with the same amount of money, but because of the choices that we make as we move around the board, we become different as far as incomes and assets are concerned. It is called income mobility. Sometimes we are rich in resources, money, and properties and other times we are less rich in resources, money, and properties. I don't say "rich" and "poor." I say rich and less rich because, if you can read this book, chances are you are already in an advanced civilization and ahead of millions or even billions of less fortunate people in the world.

In jail NO one is free and they do have a bit more equality there, but what we want is a free society, agreed? That is a discussion about Socialism and Communism and for another book. Here we are talking about personal finances and making wise decisions with the money and resources that we do receive so we can build on those good decisions seeking opportunities to further advance our visions and dreams.

Every one of us has the freedom to make different decisions and for that reason, even if we did ALL start out with the same amount of money, very quickly we all experience different "rolls of the dice" or, in this case. unequal outcomes. The media and politicians like to use these differences to divide or segment us as rich and poor.

Well the truth is I know many rich people who came from very little and some wealthy people who now have lost almost everything. That is what we mean by income mobility. A free society has income mobility, despite what the media and politicians try to tell you. Decisions that you make are very important and will directly influence your outcome. Make good choices.

Seek guidance and wisdom. Resources like this book are good tools to advance your dreams in a positive way and help you make your dreams come true. Don't get caught up in the segmenting game or pointing fingers that life isn't fair. Just focus on your vision and what you can do to advance your game piece around the board successfully.

Chapter Five

What Is Residual Income And Subscription-Based Income

Residual Income

Residual income, royalty income, and Auto Pilot income. We all know the obvious cases of royalties or Residual Income from the entertainment business where musicians and movie stars make money over and over and over for something they did just one time. Subscription-Based Income is selling a service or product over and over automatically. In this chapter we will provide you with a somewhat exhaustive list to show you how many opportunities for **Auto Pilot Income** really do exist that are obtainable for almost every person out there. Here is a list of some of the current Residual and Subscription Based business models that exist today....

Let's start with the obvious.

1.) Entertainers, actors, songwriter, authors can all create residual income streams.

2.) Real Estate owners. We will discuss rental property income at length in another book. The ins and outs can be tricky, but we can help.

3.) Sales with renewal or residual incomes: insurance, merchant service agents, giftcard Sales.

4.) Drill a gas or oil well or lease your mineral rights

5.) Invent a product or create a subscription based service, such as gym memberships, magazine subscription sellers, cleaning companies.

6.) Cell Phone Resellers

7.) Vending machines, ATMs, movie boxes, food and drink items, and cell phone buy back machines

8.) Car wash clubs subscription based

9.) Investments that pay dividends stocks or insurance investments.

10.) Become a reseller or referral agent for another company.

11.) MLMs like jewelry, candles, telecom, legal services.

12.) Storage rental

13.) Laundromats

14.) Cookware, essential oils, and other consumer-based buying clubs.

15.) Landscapers, snow removal

16.) Mobile App Reseller

17.) Plumbers' annual well service and cleaning

18.) Semi-annual gutter and downspout cleaning and roof inspection

19.) Pet sitting or dog walking service

20.) Pool cleaners equipment inspection

Auto Pilot Income

The list is really endless when you sell customers on service and free inspections. Things that need to be done monthly or several times per year are excellent for home owners.

You can research Residual Income models and Subscription-Based business models and make your adjustments from there depending on your time restraints and talents. Every person reading this book has an opportunity right now to pick a task, service, or model above and begin in your spare time making the **Auto Pilot Income** that you so badly desire. If you don't have the desire, stop here and reread the chapter on mindset and belief.

Procrastination is a killer. In his book, "See You at the Top," Zig Zigler said he was so sure that he could lose weight and write a book that he didn't even start for 30 days. Don't hesitate or procrastinate make a choice and go for it.

Remember, this is a lifelong process and the plan will work if you work the plan. In our next chapter we will discuss how we are revolutionary changing business models over to Auto Pilot models with our tools and technology. These tools can help almost any business achieve a predictable flow of cash, relieving them from the cash crunch or having to start over on sales goals every month. Proven methods can be applied to almost any business to help them convert their current business models over to Cash Flow Auto Pilot machines they want them to be.

Chapter Six

Getting Started

Here is how you can turn almost any business into **Auto Pilot Income**:

As you read in the intro, I co-founded a company called Merchant Service Center, a full service Merchant Payments company selling card acceptance privileges to businesses back in the late 90's. That company was acquired by another payments company for millions of dollars.

Since then payments have become ubiquitous in our society, yet so many people know so little about them. Sure we have credit and debit cards, smart phones, and chip cards, but many people have little or no knowledge of the non-consumer side, known as the acquiring side. This is the aspect that collects the payment and pays the business.

Think Payments

We start businesses to make money, right? The result of our efforts is to profit and have an increase. Getting our customers money easily is what it's all about. Many small startups seek out FREE SAAS, **S**oftware **A**s **A** **S**ervice products that are pay as you go services. Without mentioning any names here, some of these payments products are simple and easy to set up. They have free mobile apps and send you a free gadget to plug into your phone. The issue with products like this is that they are just pacifiers or training wheels. They are okay to start with, but you really need an exit plan to find something less expensive, more service-oriented,

Auto Pilot Income

and feature-rich if you are to gain the financial independence that you desire. You must have the proper payments acceptance methods in place.

So many small startups have huge potential, but they get stuck in a payments acceptance program that really will be like training wheels. Who really gets on a bike with the goal of *always using training wheels*? Nobody right? Most of us picture ourselves as kids riding fast and free, doing little tricks on our bike or even performing daring stunts on sketchy ramps. A little excitement and adventure is what we were seeking after. The same thinking should apply to your **Auto Pilot Income** efforts. Dream to ride fast and free, be daring and adventurous.

I am not suggesting that you be reckless. You should always follow the path of someone who has ridden the course before you, a guide if you will. In this chapter we will discuss some of the tools that others have used to blaze their trail of independence and financial freedom.

No matter what business you decide to start, try to form it in a creative way where you:

A) Offer something that people want, like, or need and

B) Give it to them at a price and at terms they can afford.

It's not always that simple or easy. The "B" Part can have some challenges as you want to offer value, but not give everything away. After all, business is about profit and profit is not a dirty word.

If someone likes, wants, and needs your product there is an opportunity to make a gross profit of higher yield, *the law of supply*

Auto Pilot Income

and demand, right? If at all possible, offer your customers terms of payment. You could use your own money, like 90 days same as cash. You could take partial payment as down payment to cover your costs and give the customer terms or time to pay on the mark up or your profit. This might mean that you have to wait a while for your profit, but if you can sell 3 times as much product then this might be a good option for you and your customers. You can also in some cases use a financial 3rd party to sell your debt to. Leasing companies and credit card issuers are always looking for partners to do business with.

Subscription Based Service

Another very popular method is to sell or market your service on a subscription basis. Car washes are good example. It used to be, your car was dirty, you went to the car wash, you bought a car wash, washed the car and it ended there.

Now a popular method is a Car Wash Club. You sign a form or subscribe via web or cell phone and you join an ongoing service. For this you get a break in price or other benefits like unlimited visits. This business model increases customer loyalty, profits, and communication and the cycle continues. It is a beautiful thing.

Cleaning companies, land scrapers, house painters, handymen, auto repair, HVAC, golf instructors, music teachers, restaurants, furniture stores, doctors, lawyers, ALL can use these methods to increase cash flow, secure income, and create a predictable **Auto Pilot Income**. These new methods are made available by the new technologies and products that we now can offer many businesses. Your next step is to allow us to give you the info you need to collect

Auto Pilot Income

payments this way. We have blazed the trail of payments. We know what products will work for you, how to market them and get your customers on board. It will take some customizing and organization on your part. Our software will help you with the fulfillment of orders and organization of shipment and returns. We recommend that you practice and perfect your ability to use these tools to truly offer the very best to your bottom line and your customers experience with your company.

Congratulations you have invested a short amount of time to get to these final steps. Coming in the next chapter will be some choices that you will need to consider.

Chapter Seven

Conclusion Or Beginning?

I hope this has been a concise informative source to help you accomplish at least these 3 things:

1) To believe that an **Auto Pilot Income** is achievable for anyone, at any age, for any job or service

2) To begin today with your vision by selecting an interest that suits your abilities and fulfills a need in your market

3) That you have found a trusted resource for assistance in building your **Auto Pilot Income** in obtaining hardware/software, legal forms, bank relationships, market and fulfillment tools to make this money appear in your bank account consistently and with little effort. That is us.

We have the knowledge and tools available for those who are interested in developing their **Auto Pilot Income** vision into a reality.

Go now to http://www.allcardusa.com/autopilotform to get started.

By consulting our team to discuss your vision and develop a plan of action to begin billing customers now, you will have made an essential and necessary step to achieving your dreams. These tools are available to you from our list of proven partners. These technologies will channel money into your bank account.

Some first questions to ask yourself are:

Auto Pilot Income

1. Have you registered a fictitious name with the state where your business will be?

2. Have you obtained an EIN number from the IRS?

3. Have you opened your business checking account?

These are 3 things that you should have before we begin. If you have questions regarding these steps please seek out these resources in your state and states that you plan to conduct business in. In the United States look for the Secretary of State in your home state for more direction. Outside the U.S. seek direction from your local government first. Disclaimer, this is not a substitute for the advice of a professional in your area. For IRS info on obtaining an EIN go to IRS.gov.

This final chapter is titled Conclusion or Beginning. That outcome depends on what you do with this call to action.

We believe that you were created on purpose for a purpose. We believe in you and your potential to be profitable and productive. Now you must believe in yourself and take this to the next level. Are you ready to begin?

Go now to http://www.allcardusa.com/autopilotform to get started.